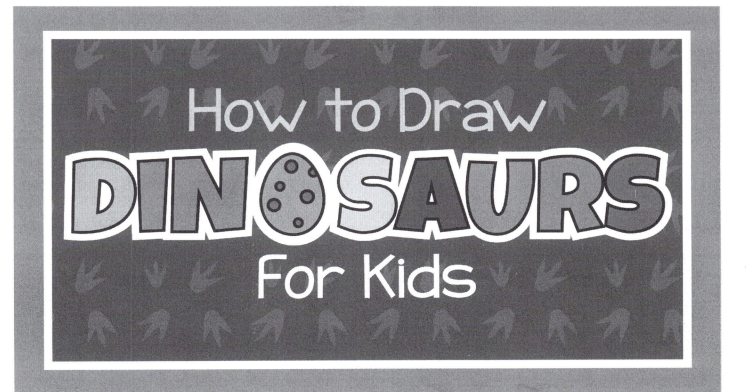

This book belongs to:

Finlay Galloway

Table of Contents

Tyrannosaurus rex 6

Triceratops 8

Brachiosaurus 10

Spinosaurus 12

Velociraptor 14

Allosaurus 16

Ankylosaurus 18

Kentrosaurus 20

Dracorex 22

Diplodocus 24

Table of Contents

Brontosaurus 26

Carnotaurus 28

Parasaurolophus 30

Stegosaurus 32

Pterodactylus 34

Oviraptor.............................. 36

Apatosaurus 38

Dilophosaurus 40

Iguanodon 42

Coelophysis 44

Table of Contents

Archaeopteryx 46

Pteranodon 48

Mosasaurus 50

Argentinosaurus 52

Deinonychus 54

Giganotosaurus 56

Baryonyx 58

Plesiosaurus 60

Pachycephalosaurus 62

Therizinosaurus 64

Table of Contents

Xenoceratops 66

Styracosaurus 68

Silvisaurus 70

Lirainosaurus 72

Gallimimus 74

Ichthyosaurus 76

Europasaurus 78

Tsintaosaurus 80

Gastornis 82

Dimetrodon 84

Tyrannosaurus rex

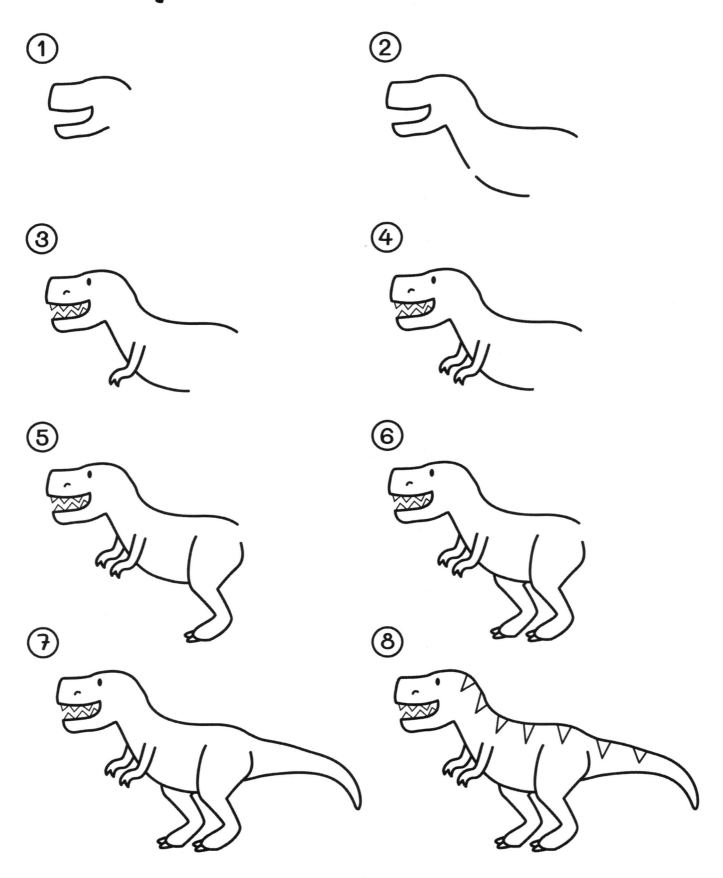

Now it's your turn!

Triceratops

Now it's your turn!

Brachiosaurus

Now it's your turn!

Spinosaurus

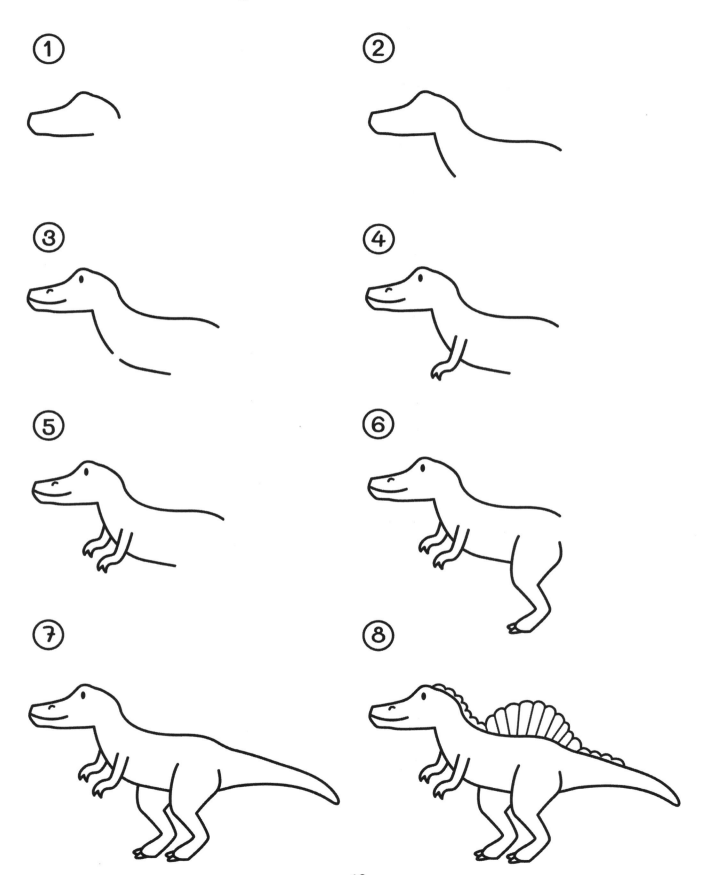

Now it's your turn!

Velociraptor

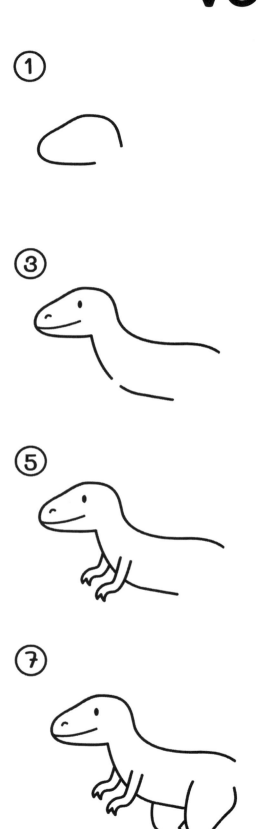
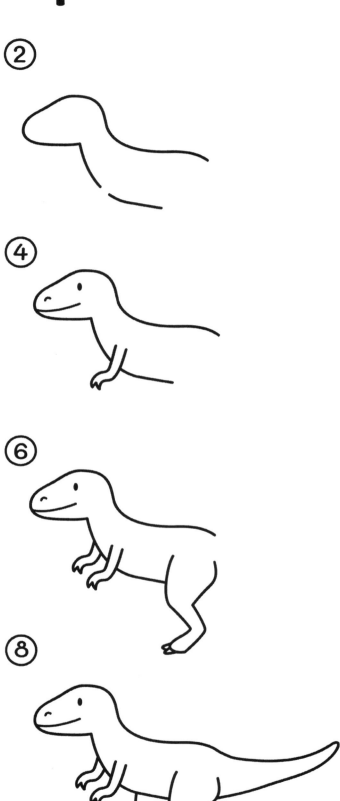

Now it's your turn!

Allosaurus

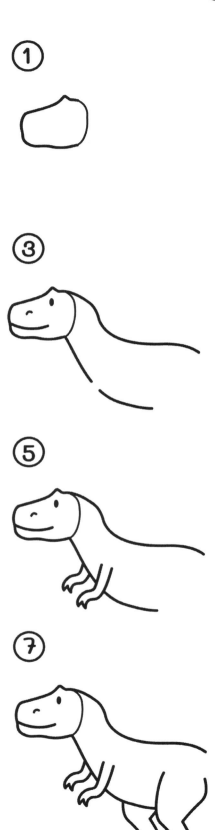
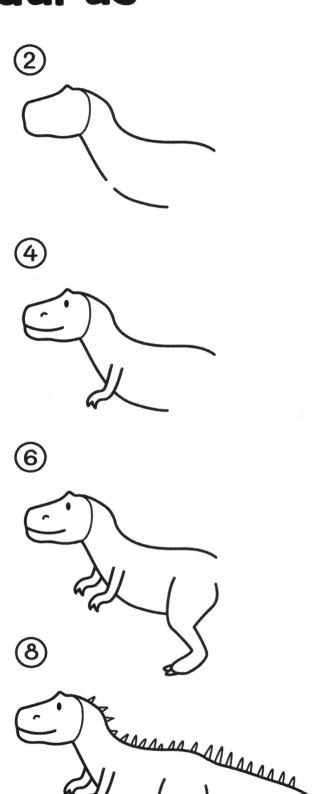

Now it's your turn!

Ankylosaurus

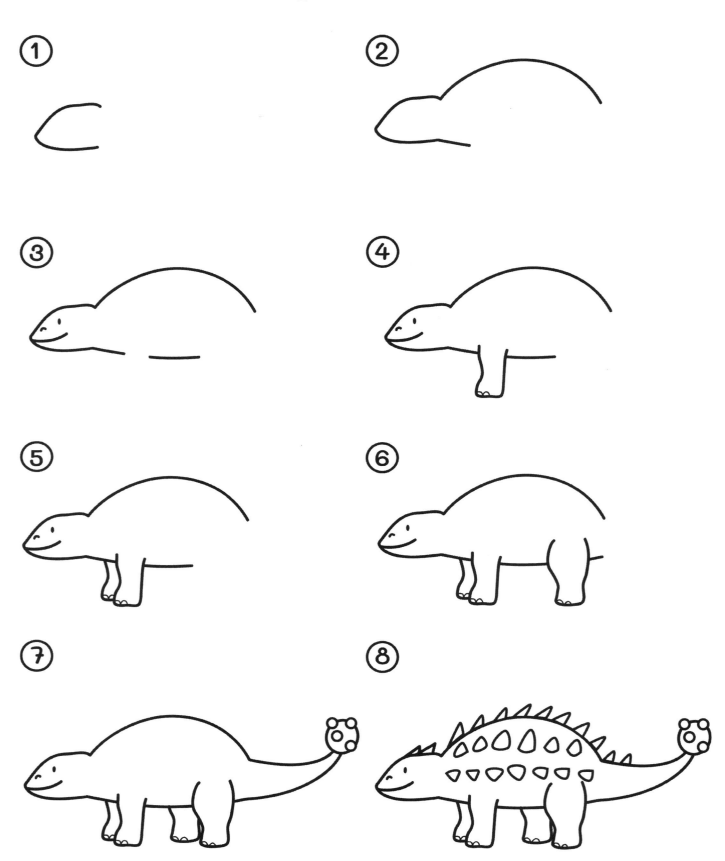

Now it's your turn!

Kentrosaurus

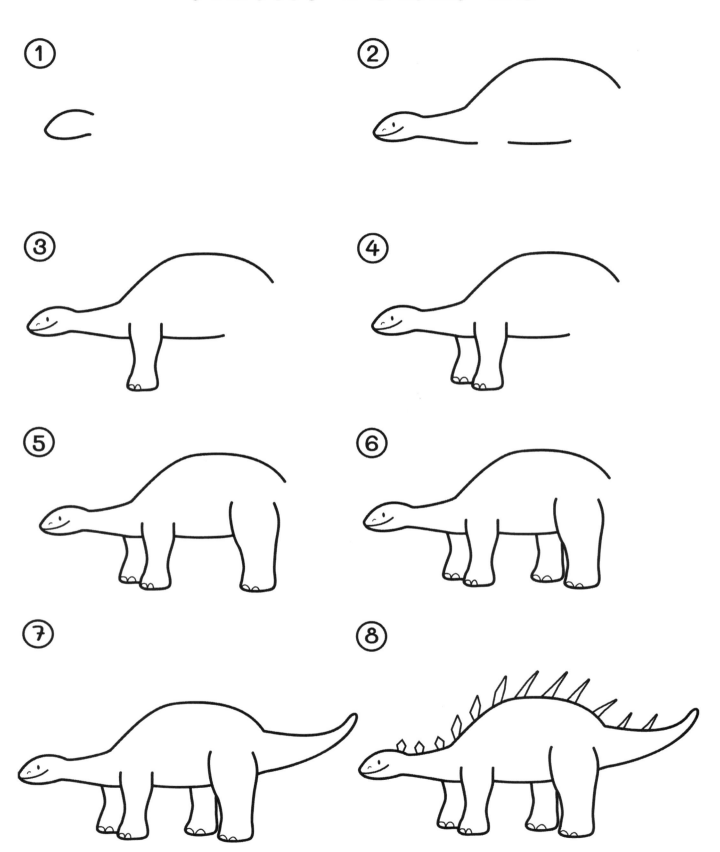

Now it's your turn!

Dracorex

①

②

③

④

⑤

⑥

⑦

⑧

Now it's your turn!

Diplodocus

Now it's your turn!

Brontosaurus

Now it's your turn!

Carnotaurus

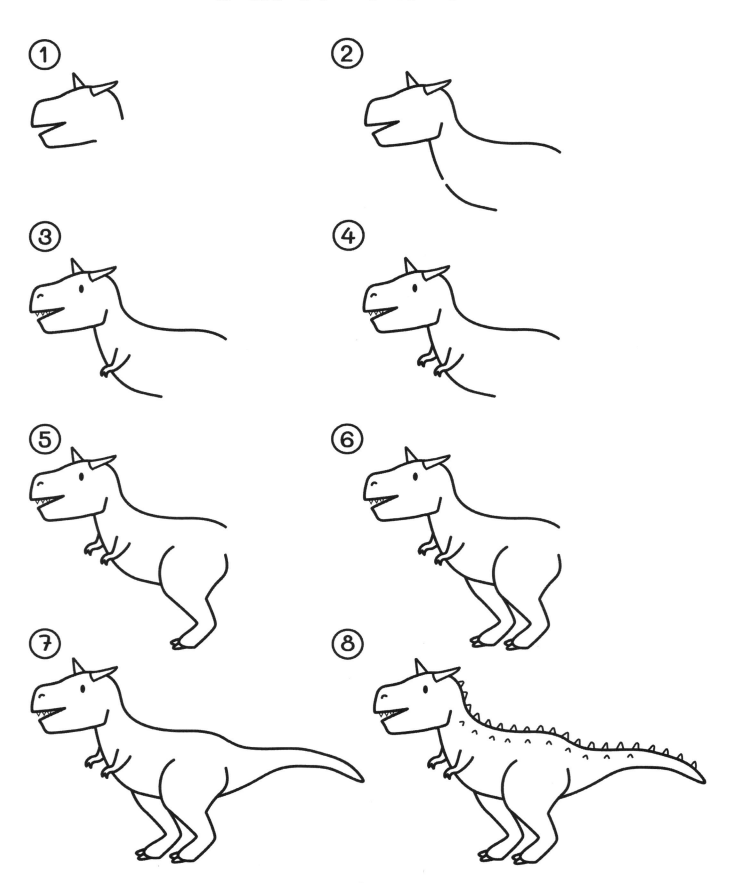

Now it's your turn!

Parasaurolophus

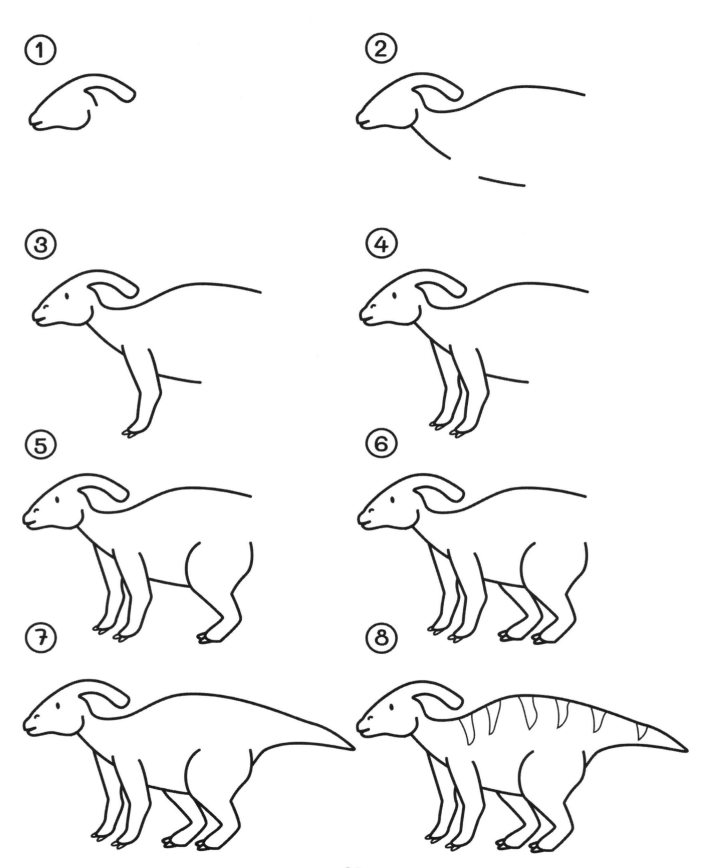

Now it's your turn!

Stegosaurus

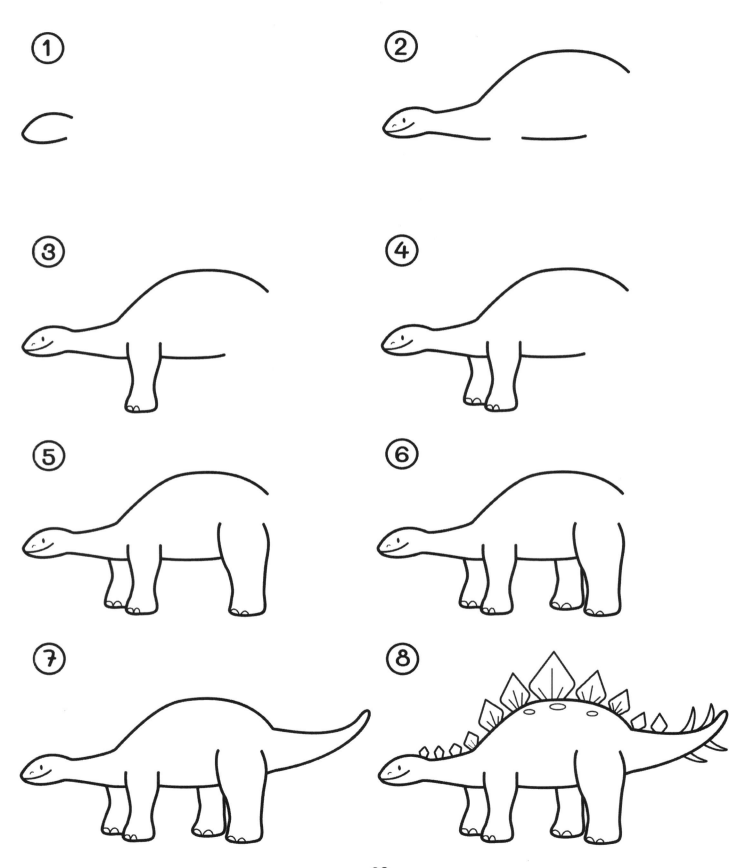

Now it's your turn!

Pterodactylus

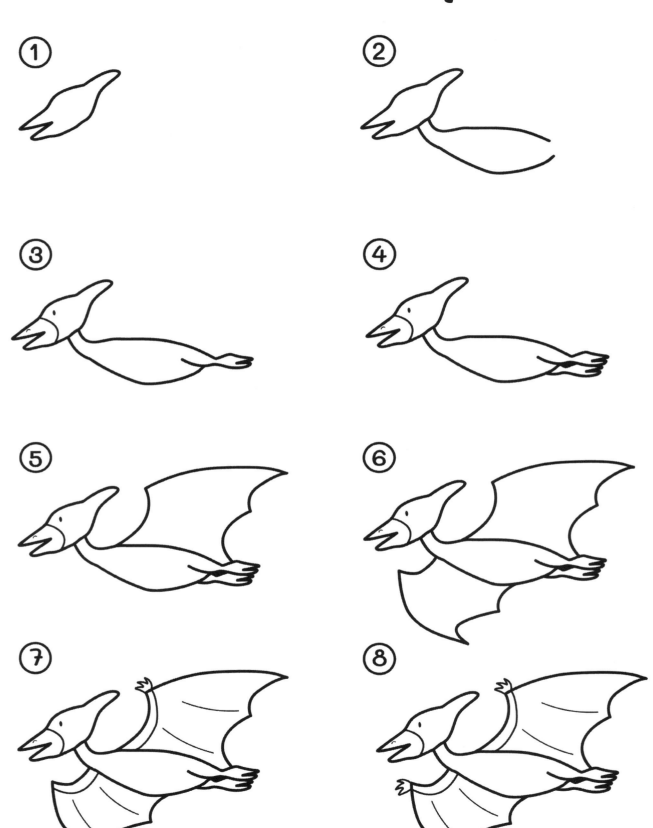

Now it's your turn!

Oviraptor

Now it's your turn!

Apatosaurus

Now it's your turn!

Dilophosaurus

Now it's your turn!

Iguanodon

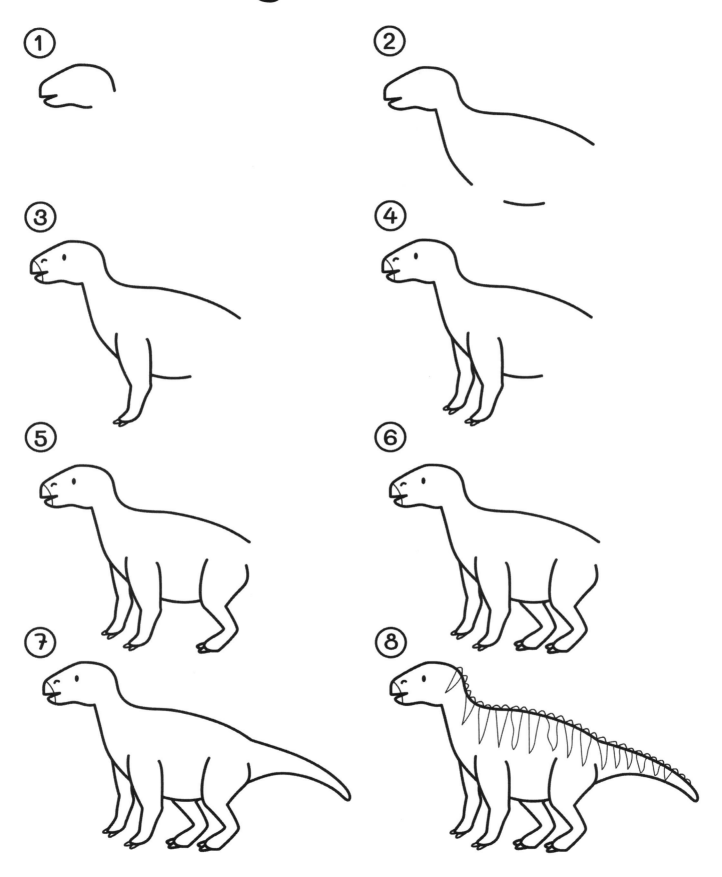

Now it's your turn!

Coelophysis

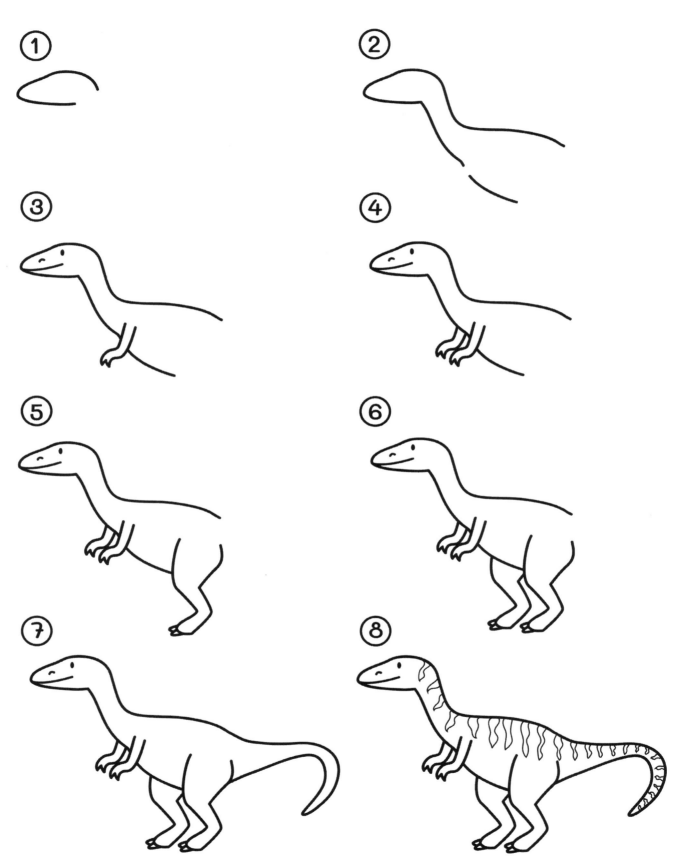

Now it's your turn!

Archaeopteryx

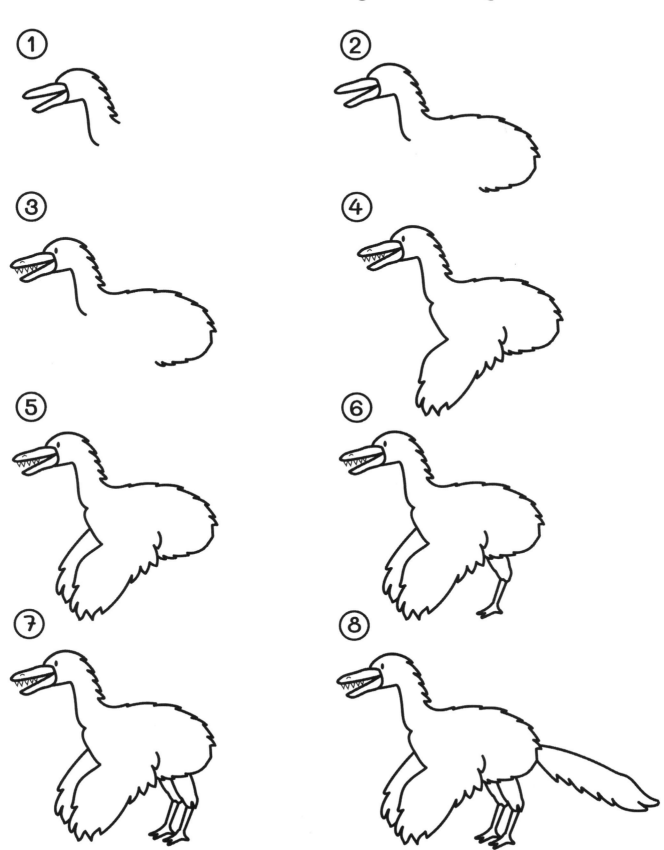

Now it's your turn!

Pteranodon

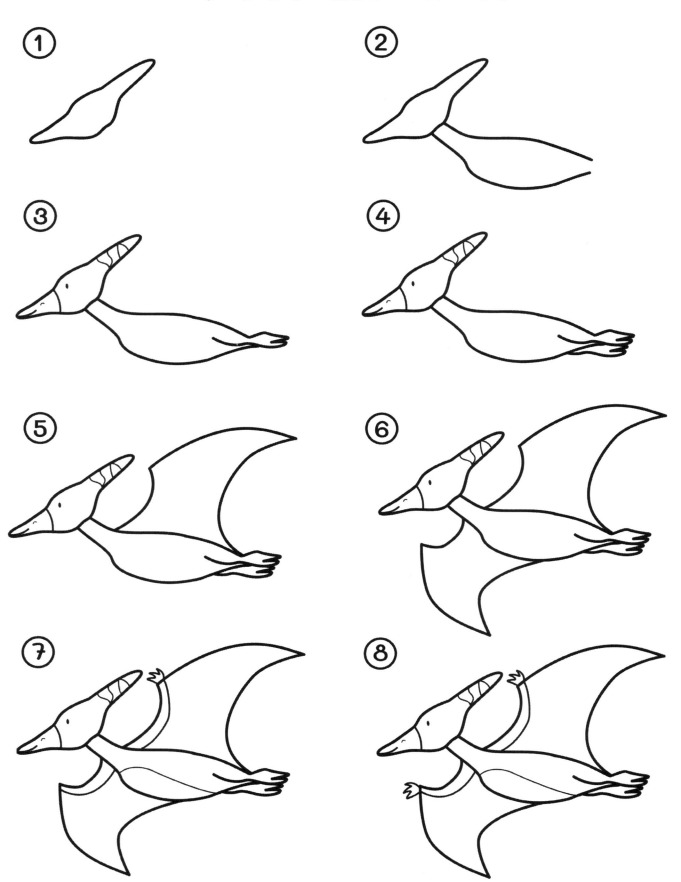

Now it's your turn!

Mosasaurus

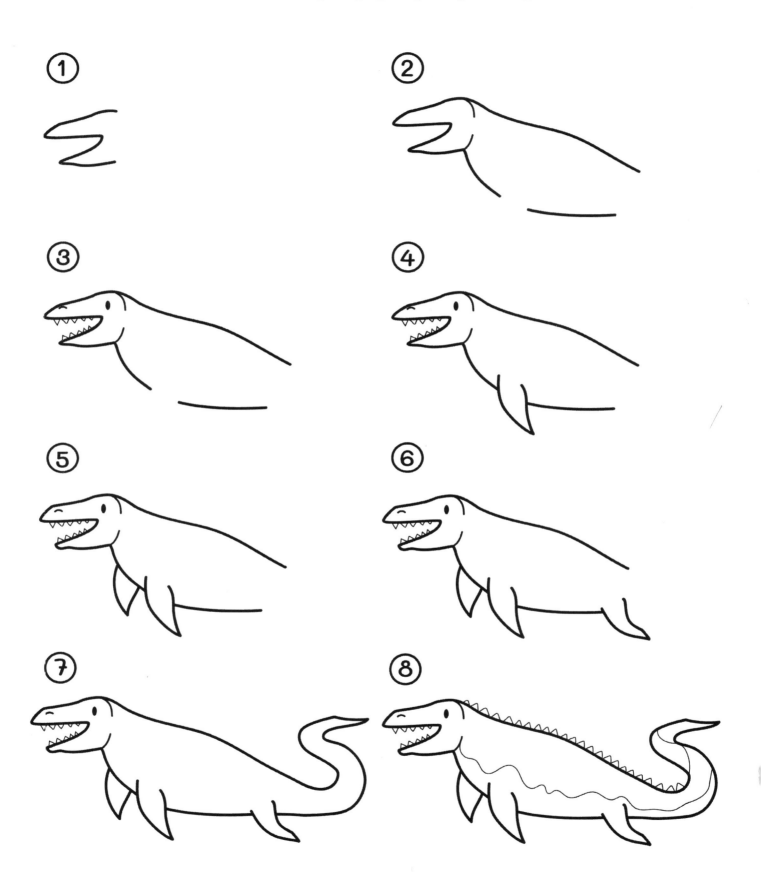

Now it's your turn!

Argentinosaurus

Now it's your turn!

Deinonychus

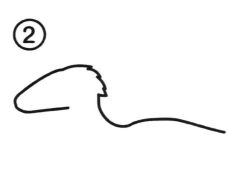
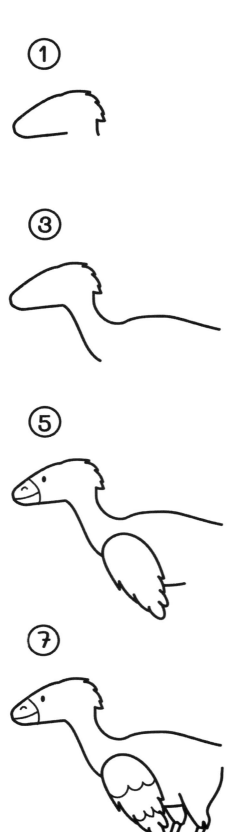
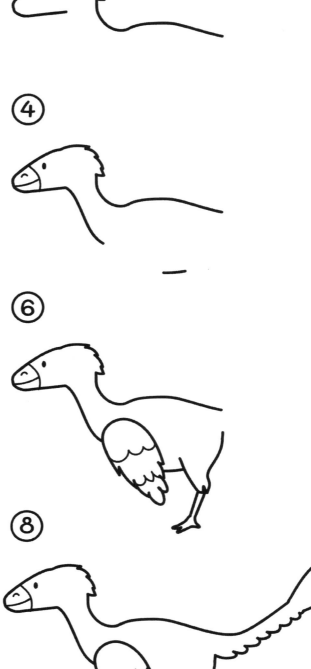

Now it's your turn!

Giganotosaurus

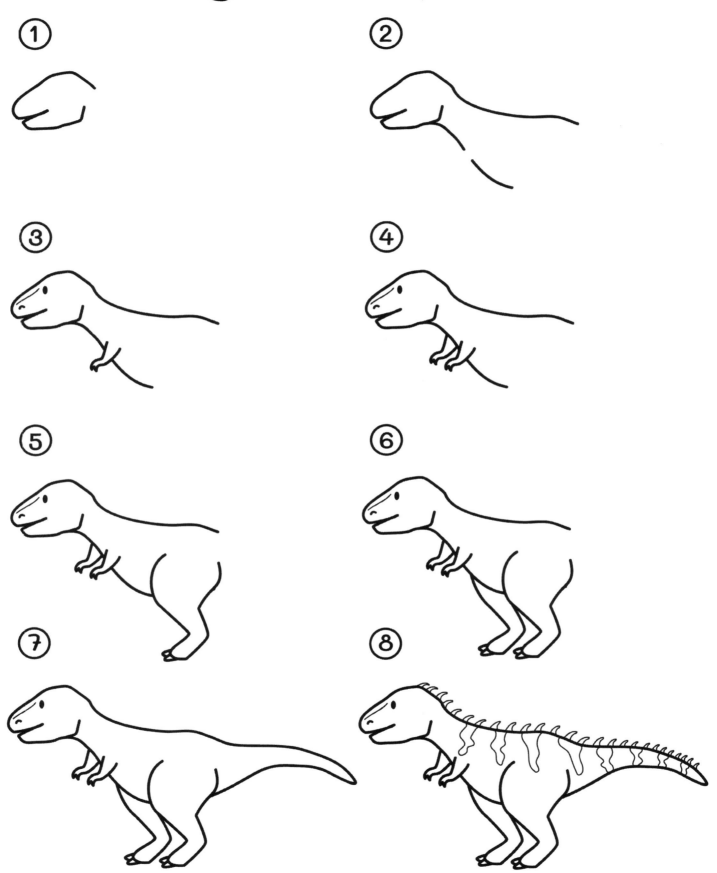

Now it's your turn!

Baryonyx

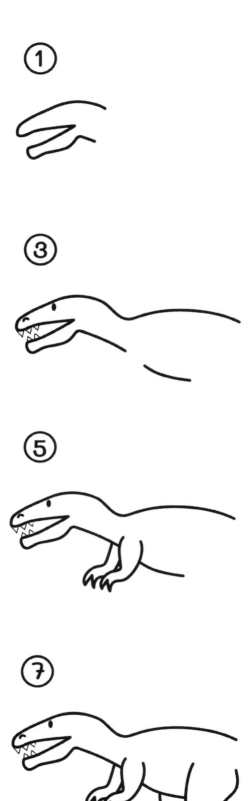
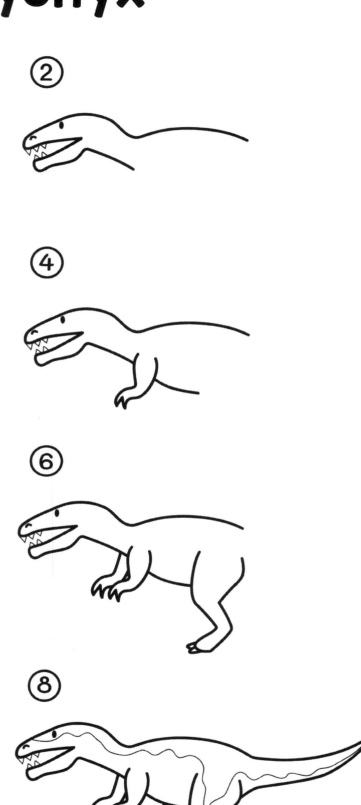

Now it's your turn!

Plesiosaurus

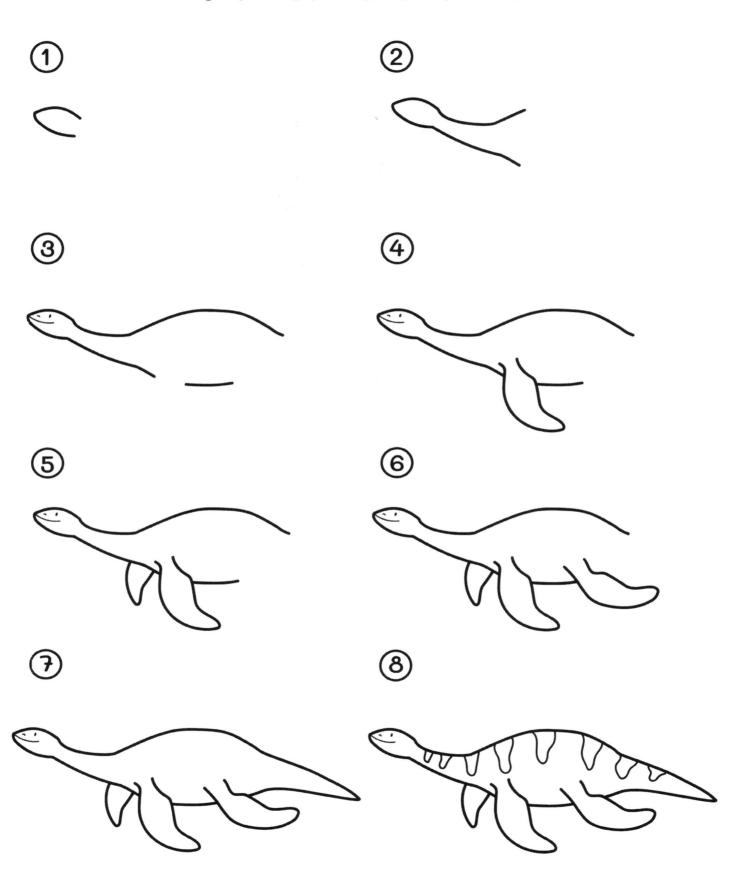

Now it's your turn!

Pachycephalosaurus

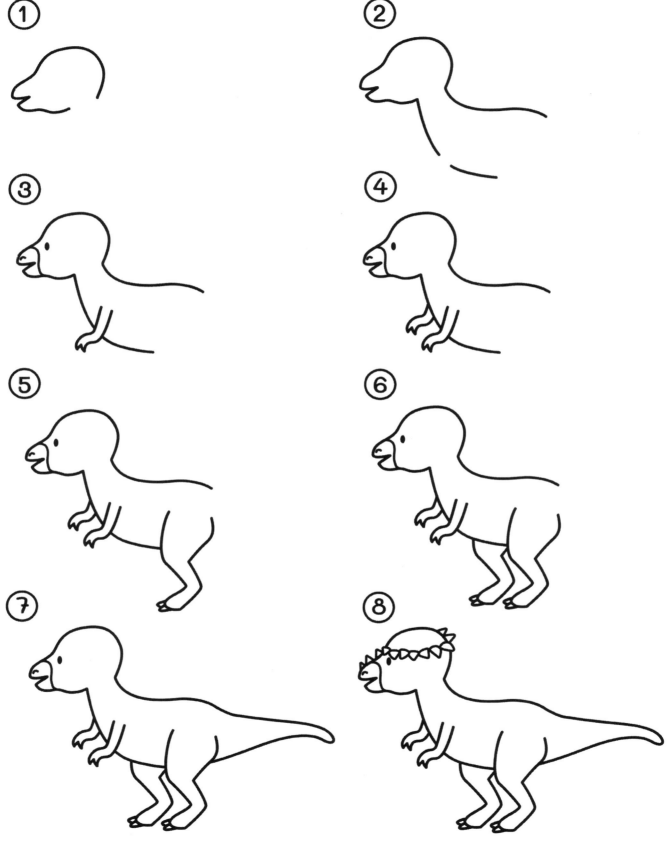

Now it's your turn!

Therizinosaurus

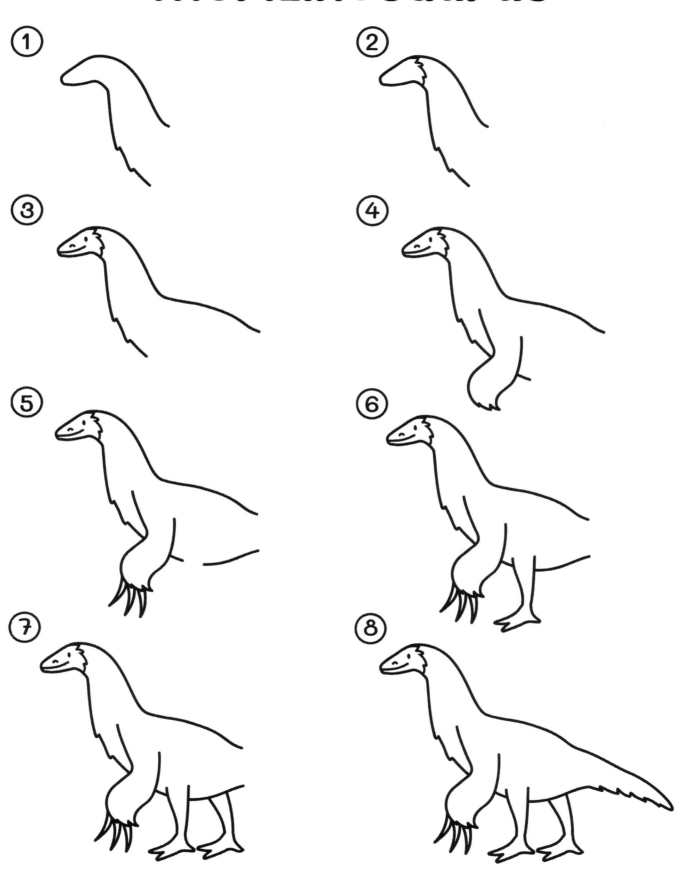

Now it's your turn!

Xenoceratops

Now it's your turn!

Styracosaurus

Now it's your turn!

Silvisaurus

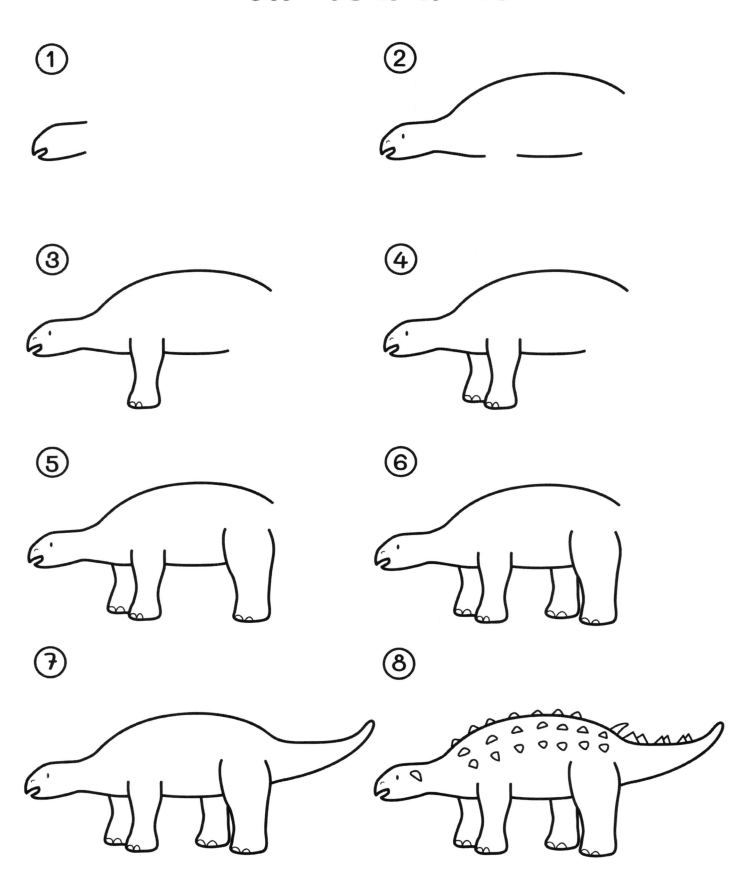

Now it's your turn!

Lirainosaurus

Now it's your turn!

Gallimimus

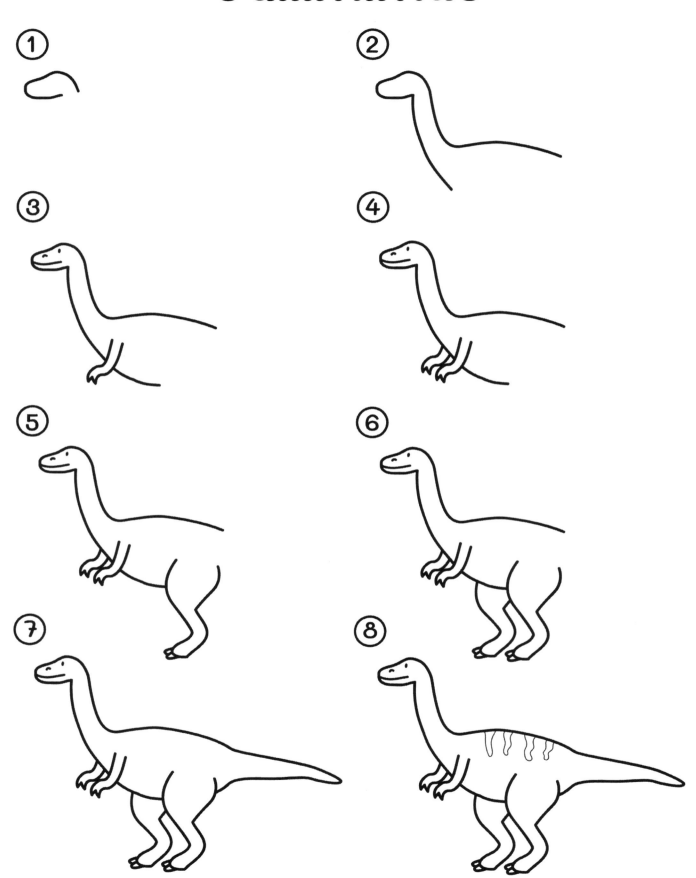

Now it's your turn!

Ichthyosaurus

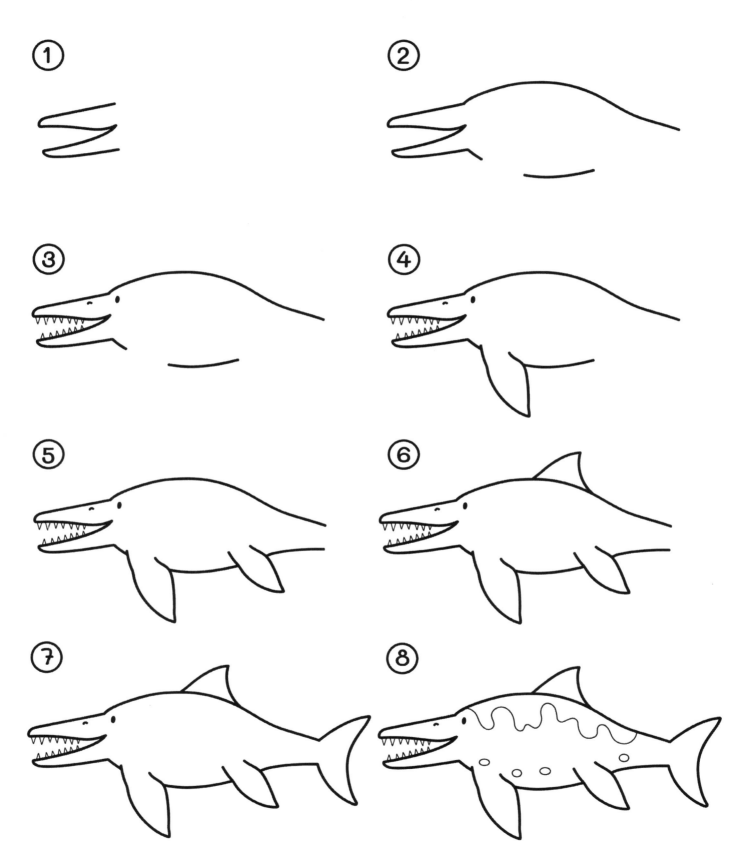

Now it's your turn!

Europasaurus

Now it's your turn!

Tsintaosaurus

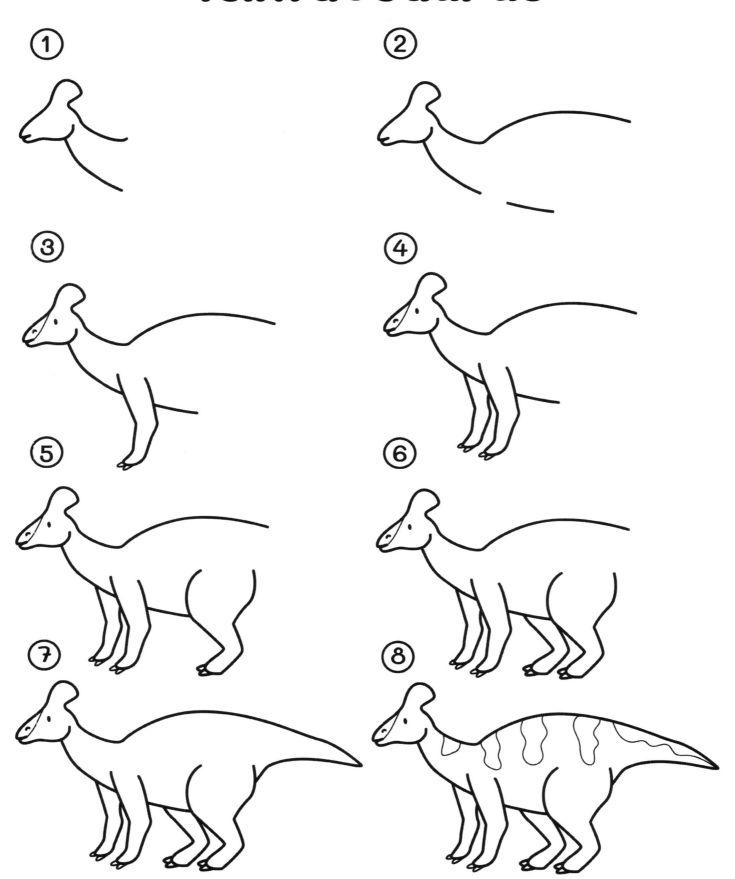

Now it's your turn!

Gastornis

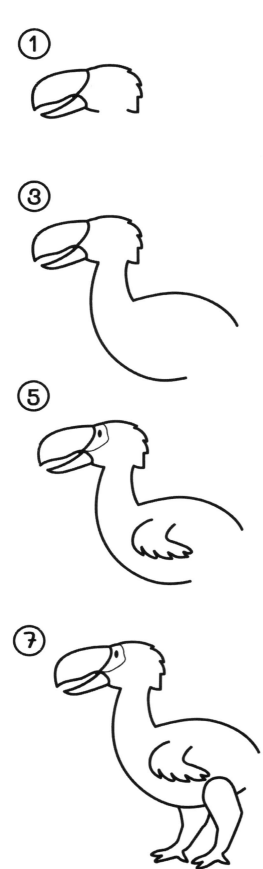

Now it's your turn!

Dimetrodon

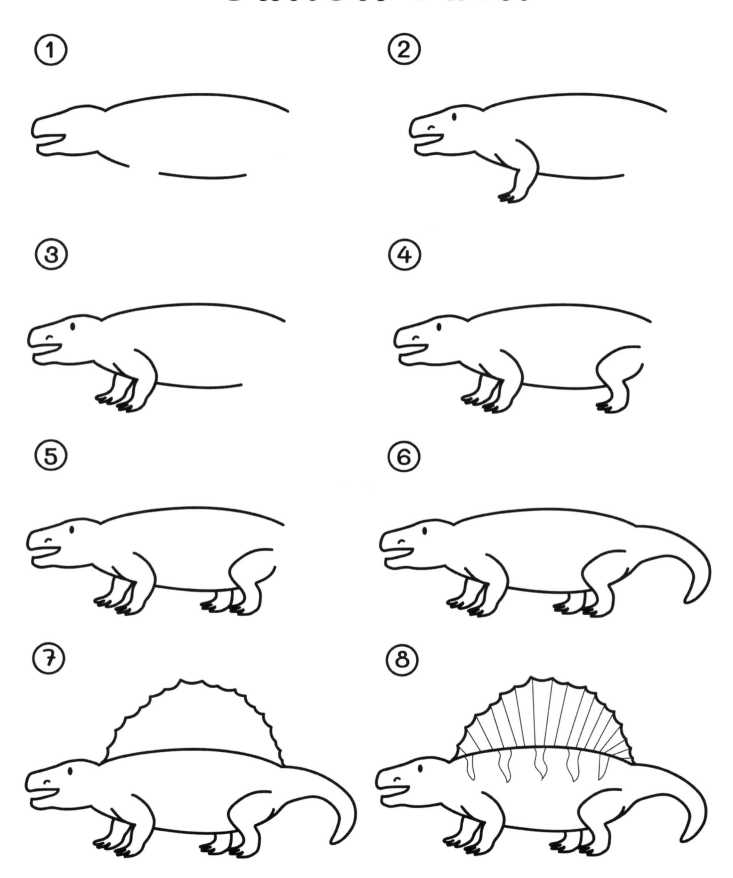

Now it's your turn!

...HOPE YOU HAD A GREAT TIME WITH US...

We would be happy to color with you again soon.

It would be amazing if you wrote an honest product review on Amazon. It only takes 1-2 minutes and means a lot to us!

QUESTIONS, REQUESTS, OR FEEDBACK?

Write us an email: baldehmarketing@gmail.com

Printed in Great Britain
by Amazon

10836664R00050